GUIDED BY ANGELS

Breast Cancer? Not Now

Heather Macdonald

BALBOA.
PRESS

A DIVISION OF HAY HOUSE

Balboa Press books may be ordered through booksellers or by contacting:

Balboa Press
A Division of Hay House
1663 Liberty Drive
Bloomington, IN 47403
www.balboapress.com.au
1 (877) 407-4847

Print information available on the last page.

ISBN: 978-1-5043-0764-2 (sc)
ISBN: 978-1-5043-0765-9 (e)

Balboa Press rev. date: 04/07/2017

Out of suffering have emerged the strongest souls.
The most massive characters are seemed with scars.

E.H. Chapin (1814–1880)

Contents

Acknowledgements

To all those before me who have taken a similar journey.

To all my ancestors and the angels, who carried me through such a highly charged roller coaster of emotions whilst on such a challenging journey.

To my family and friends, who helped and supported me physically and emotionally.

To colleagues who gave me encouragement.

To those who took part in my care.

I thank each and every one from the bottom of my heart.

Epigraph reasoning

Throughout the book, I have famous quotes situated in areas where they meant a lot to me. They are situated in places which had particular meaning for me at the time.

These quotes helped me focus on staying positive. I feel that they also aided the healing process.

Introduction

> You have to accept whatever comes and the only important thing is that you meet it with courage and the best you have to give.
>
> Eleanor Roosevelt (1884 – 1962)

Born into pioneering families and growing up on the banks of the Tully River, where the man-eating crocodiles roam free, was a challenge. There were also dingoes, among other scary things. When we were young, one would not go outside alone at night.

My parents were spiritual which followed through with the family.

As a young woman, I had my heart set on being an airline attendant. All I had to do was one year of nursing to be eligible to apply. This brought me to an arena where as to complete nursing studies. Years later, when I did apply to be an airline attendant one had to be at least fluent bilingual – which I was not. I had sufficient to get me by for traveling, but insufficient for the position. I continued with my nursing career which eventually led me to work overseas.

As a single mother, I raised my children unaided.

My daughter Maree an asthmatic, my son Mike has cystic fibrosis, and I myself have a thyroid condition, plus I work full time as a registered nurse; my work was cut out for me.

I had been told that my Mike would be lucky to live past three years of age. My response was, "Over my dead body!"

He is currently thirty-seven years old and is doing quite well.

My dedication to his treatment and as wholesome a diet as I could afford pulled us through.

Being a spiritualist and registered nurse, our pathway was paved.

The strain was tremendous, leaving me mentally and physically exhausted.

At the age of forty-five, my children now of voting age, my life was about to change. In fact, I made a decision that would possibly be one of the biggest in my life.

During my career, I worked around Australia and abroad. London was my home for four years; during this time, I travelled extensively.

Initially, I found it difficult to settle back into Queensland, so I lived in Perth W.A. for seven years. I did a solo drive around Australia in 2005 (in my Mazda 323) from Perth (going north, across then around). I then drove back to Queensland again in 2007.

With grandchildren in the making, I returned to Queensland, settling near Brisbane.

I have been through a lot of scenarios and challenges, but this current challenge has tested me more than I could ever imagine.

I spent my life caring for others, often times putting myself second; I neglected my own health checks and needs.

In November 2015, I noticed that my left nipple was inverted. The mammogram and ultrasound were inconclusive, which meant further investigation.

A biopsy was taken on November 30, with results on December 3; surgical appointment was on December 7; the mastectomy was performed December 9, and then axillary clearance was done on December 17.

The youngest of nine siblings, Margaret had died three years earlier, due to ovarian cancer. I was the seventh born of the nine. The four brothers - Alfred, David, Andrew and Duncan were born first in order as written. Then the five sisters – Eileen, Jeanette, Heather, Irene and Margaret in order as written.

On December 4, I informed my children Maree and Mike, but was still unable to give answers to all their questions.

Maree, a mother of three children, Leigh, Mae and Xander. Mae being wheelchair bound is fully dependant; I usually helped where possible.

Myself, I knew I would find it difficult to inform the family. It had to be done; I did it after seeing the surgeon on December 7.

My mother had the same surgery many years ago, as did her mother.

The song, "Don't Worry Be Happy," had not long hit the charts in Australia when Mum was diagnosed. This became her theme song; she lived a further twenty years.

To inform my siblings, I sang the song; they knew instantly. I then rang my cousin, who had also been through the surgery. I told her that I was joining the club, that of her and Mum; she also knew instantly. My siblings informed my Aunt Elsie and Uncle Wal (Mum's siblings.)

Being a Reiki Master and SKHM Master, I had paid to do a workshop with Patrick Zeigler (founder of SKHM); this was now not possible. I was refunded my money and have since been informed that he is returning to Australia, so I have rebooked to do the workshop.

Reiki and SKHM (Seichim) are both forms of healing energies.

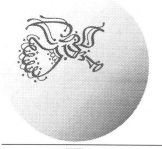

The Diagnosis

Dream 1 (Lesson 1)

In late April 2015, I experienced a very disturbing dream.

In the dream, I was with my late sister Margaret, her husband Hugh, and their youngest son Wayne (who is intellectually disadvantaged).

We had been inside a massive marble building.

No one spoke. I felt ill, just knowing that I had been condemned, but I didn't know the reason. The burden of what-ever it was, made me feel sick to the stomach.

I woke crying and sobbing my heart out. I couldn't go back to sleep.

I sobbed on and off for the next week or so.

For the life of me, I could not understand the dream. I ran it through my mind over and over trying to decipher the meaning.

I could not understand why it disturbed me the way it did as nothing really happened in the dream, apart from the "deathly' silence.

I now put this dream down to the cancer, having visited the Hall of Records. I must have been shown my fate, though that was not in my dream – which leaves it open to have the outcome altered.

> *Every area of trouble gives out a ray of hope,*
> *and the one unchangeable certainty*
> *is that nothing*
> *is certain or unchangeable.*
>
> *John F. Kennedy (1917–1963)*

Dream 2 (Lesson 2)

In May 2015, I had another extremely disturbing dream. This one was much more disturbing.

I was with my son-in-law Alex and daughter Maree.

We walked silently through a long tunnel made of rocks. We came to a viewing window where two people (one man and one woman, with others in the distance) were seated on a disc with their feet tucked toward their bottom. I lost focus on the man as I recognised the woman.

She was me, looking right back at me.

They were in a furnace, and the discs were rotating. They had no skin or hair. I felt ill looking through this viewing window, as there were body parts here and there. I made a comment regarding this, saying that they will surely die in there. Alex replied that they would be fine.

I kept looking at myself in the furnace, and she just sat still, looking back at me. I started to cry.

I woke crying, sobbing harder and longer than I did over the previous dream.

I remained awake until dawn due to the effect the dream had on me. I decided to have breakfast and return to bed when I finally was able to drift off to sleep, only to wake crying yet again.

Again, I cried on and off over the coming weeks, just thinking of the dreams, trying to decipher them became an endless battle.

To get them out of my head, I decided that they must have been from past lives.

I now put this dream down to radiation; the body parts were of people with cancer who didn't live through the treatment.

Reading (Lesson 3)

I had done a card (Tarot) reading on myself some time back which was in monthly lots, for twelve months ahead; the main theme of the reading was that I would get news which would affect the whole family; I would also take a very long mental and physical journey; there was the making of contracts and then have them dissolved – all so very confusing.

Winter came and went, and I noticed that my left nipple was inverted.

During the cooler months, I had noticed a discrepancy but put it down to the cool air; now, it was too obvious to ignore.

A lump was also palpable, putting a chill up my spine, as it was not just the fact that it was there, but also how big it was (it was also very hard.)

I got in for an appointment a week later and then booked a mammogram and ultrasound both were inconclusive.

The Biopsy

The biopsy was taken on 30 November. It was very, very painful. It only took a short time but left me with an ache that lasted a few days.

The doctor said that the specimen was difficult to take, as the lump was so very hard.

After a local anaesthetic, a tiny incision was made, a cylinder about thirty centimetres long takes a piece of tissue with claws that snap out after a trigger is pulled.

The great virtue in life is real courage that knows how to face facts and live beyond them.

D.H. Lawrence (1885–1930)

Reading (Lesson 4)

Going back to my notebook, where I had recorded the card reading a few months earlier, I could now see what was going to affect the whole family. I still believed all would be well, but I could not understand the part of the reading, which left me feeling frustrated and tied down, nor could I understand taking a very long physical and mental journey. I was also to have new opportunities, the cards said, but forces were working against me. I now see that the contracts would be made with my doctors which would later dissolve when no longer requiring their care. It would also include hospital visits, as these are actually signed contracts giving healthcare workers permission to do their duty, these have to be renewed on each admission.

I knew that I would have to have a lumpectomy or mastectomy at the most; this was how my thoughts were going.

I could not see myself requiring any further treatment, as my mother had no further treatment. It seemed that I was in complete denial.

The Cat

I had seen an advertisement in the local paper about a cat available for adoption from the local animal shelter. I went to visit the cat. She reminded me a little of my previous cat. As I stroked her, she rubbed against my hand.

They would only hold her for a week. She was reported to be an unfriendly cat, not getting on with other animals and not warming to visitors, especially children. I told her quietly that I would come back to get her and not to go with someone else, because I had no other pets apart from goldfish.

That evening, I rang Maree and asked to borrow her animal-transport cage.

Biopsy Results

The GP rang me at home on the morning of 3 December, asking me to come and see her.

As it was her day off, I knew that the news was not good; face to face with an appointment, is how this news is delivered. The result was positive, > 95 percent, invasive lobular cancer. I felt so dirty. I wanted it gone already.

I left my GP with a plan of action going through my mind. My first priority was to tell Mike and Maree and my manager (Ashley) at work. I decided to leave early for work, calling in at Maree's place first. She had been unaware of what had been taking place. She was at a friend's place; her mother-in-law Rita and Xander were at home. I stayed with Rita and Xander for about an hour, playing with our grandson while conversing with Rita. I never revealed the reason for my visit to Rita.

My mind was a blur, and I forgot to get the pet-transport cage.

When it became apparent that Maree would not be home any time soon, I excused myself and left for work.

On arrival to work, I spoke privately to my manager Ashley to sort out my options and to arrange time off. Four weeks sick leave was available as I rarely have sick days. Also, I had four weeks of annual leave – holiday plans for Winton and Longreach now on hold (ancestors from both of my parent's families are in the Stockman's Hall of Fame at Longreach) and I had been planning this visit for quite some time as it meant so much to me.

The following day, I called in at Maree's on my way to work. She was very chatty and asked if I had forgotten the pet cage. I told her I had; she seemed surprised and put it in my car. I followed her around while talking. I was wondering when I would be able to get to speak as she was full of news.

Eventually, I told her to sit down, as I needed to talk. I sat but she stood, waiting as though she realized that I had something shocking to say. As I told her my news, she went quiet and looked at me. She asked why I had said nothing earlier.

Initially, I stayed silent as it may have been benign – I was hoping at least. I had said that I did not want her worrying needlessly. I told her that I had to tell her in person, not on the phone. I was taught we were to give this type of news in person.

She appeared frozen for a minute and then started pacing. I answered her questions and told her that I would know more after seeing the surgeon. We hugged tight, and I told her I had no plans on meeting my Maker just yet. I was relieved to have finally told her but felt sick in the stomach, yet I managed to go to work and stay focused.

I told my colleagues at work, one on one, when I got the chance. I wanted them to hear it from myself.

After my shift ended, my journey began.

Healing

During the past weeks, I had prayed in earnest and done Reiki and SKHM healing on myself. I had asked the Angels and Masters and all masters of all styles of healing from the Light to heal my whole physical and spiritual being, to rid my body of this cancerous growth.

One evening, a pale blue healing light shot right through me, from my head to feet, causing a jolt.

A voice then told me that this was what I had asked for.

I knew then that I would get through this.

Turn your face to the sun and the shadows fall behind you.

Maori Proverb

The Surgery

Everything was so surreal; the surgeon had viewed the results and was examining my body. As with the GP, she got straight to the point.

We discussed whether I should have a lumpectomy, mastectomy, or mastectomy/clearance, and then I signed a consent form for a mastectomy plus sentinel node for 9 December—the same date that my cousin Jane had it done ten years earlier.

My biggest concern was how I was going to continue paying the mortgage and bills, thus keeping a roof over my head.

Even though I had seen the surgeon at one hospital, the only theatre time she could get was at another hospital. With the procedure being urgent, I was first on the morning list of Wednesday, 9 December, 2015.

On leaving the surgeon, I went to purchase all that I would need before collecting the cat. Then, on getting home, I started informing my siblings.

"Here's a little song I wrote,

You might want to sing it note for note.

Don't worry, be happy."

My eldest (Eileen) sister said, "That's what Mum sang when she had her mastectomy." With tears in my eyes, I told her I had joined that same club.

I rang another two siblings but then had no courage left, so I asked them to pass the information onto the others.

I rang my cousin Jane, who had a mastectomy ten years earlier, and told her that I was joining the same club as her and Mum.

Having arranged Mike to care for the cat while I was in having surgery, I went to collect her from the animal shelter on 8 December.

The Cat

The advertisement in the newspaper had read:

"Fluffy Pocahontas needs home," along with a photo of her.

We would be warriors together. Being a tortoise shell, she has excellent camouflage, making it difficult to locate her. I discovered that she had a fear of children and dogs; she was a very nervous cat.

It took a couple of weeks for her to relax enough to settle in. Now she is like my second shadow.

The cat (who I simply call Puss) hid when I got her home. I let her settle in, in her own way. As I had an appointment to attend, I left her hiding behind the cushions.

Contrast Injection

The morning before my surgery, I checked in at the radiology lab to have an injection of contrast. I had been warned that it would be painful.

While lying on the table, slightly anxious, the staff prepared the injection while telling me what would be done. They told me that I was free to express my pain how I chose, whether it be call out, cry, or scream - most scream she said.

She proceeded to inject the contrast at six o'clock of my left nipple.

I tried to contain myself, but I moaned and yelled.

The process was now for me to massage the dye around the breast for the next hour or so; it had to be done vigorously. The dye goes to all affected tissue, also highlighting the sentinel node.

This was not only very trying, I was exhausted but had to continue. My arms ached, having to continue I tried to alternate; resting one then the other, it caused excruciating pain.

Eventually, the radiographers were satisfied that sufficient massaging had been done.

The pain continued throughout the night. Due to the pain, my breast felt double the size. Eventually, I drifted off to sleep.

Dream 3 (Lesson 6)

I had another nightmare where I was resisting a very evil seducer who was very strong and determined. He was tall and slim with dark hair, olive complexion, and unusually long, spindly fingers. He was salivating and had a menacing look about him, also with vile breath and long pointed tongue. I managed to escape somehow, but my left breast was tarnished in the process. I interpreted the seducer as being the cancerous growth.

This was another confirmation that I would beat this.

Phone calls from near and far came wishing me well, though I knew they were worried by the tone of their voice. My mind was spinning so took a long soak in the bath then proceeded to do some relaxing exercises in the form of breathing and visual meditation. It was difficult, so I tried one visual experience after the other. With candles lit in my prayer room, I concentrated on Margaret, Mum, Dad and others. I prayed with all my might that all will be well. I felt a warm buzz around me, I knew that they were there holding me.

Feeling more relaxed, I made tea and toast as I was fasting from food and drink from midnight. (fasting is essential prior to any general anaesthetic, this is usually from six hours prior to the surgery.)

First Surgery

I was up at 04.30 and went into the shower, fed Puss and took a taxi to the hospital. It felt like I was living a nightmare, being up at this hour heading for my surgery.

Was this really happening?

Before long, I was admitted and in theatre attire; they performed an ECG, and I was on my way.

A very gentle anaesthetist came and asked the usual questions. I broke down as I revealed to her how I had awareness during my thyroidectomy in 1994.

(Even though I had been paralysed, with drugs, and ventilated, I was awake for the first part of the procedure during my thyroidectomy – monitors alarming alerted the staff.) Before anything else, she put an awareness probe (attached to a monitor) on my forehead.

When I arrived onto the ward, lunch was being served. I felt relaxed and comfortable; I knew where I was as I saw the tubes, but felt no pain.

I rang my manager Ashley at work after the procedure, and she was surprised but glad to hear from me. I told her that the evil twin was in the bin and thanked the staff for the flowers. She told me I needed to make the "evil twin" into a verse.

Evil Twin

The evil twin …
now in the bin.
Oh, to be rid of that thing,
my heart does sing.
Care for one self,
return to health.
Life in Plan B,
the new life for me.

Results

Six nodes had been taken along with the full mastectomy; three nodes were affected. These nodes had picked up the dye and had to be removed also.

I rarely took pain tablets or drank alcohol and so am very sensitive to such things. After I was given a tablet for pain, my blood pressure dropped, and my bed had to be tilted and blood pressure monitored.

To keep my oxygen levels normal, I did deep breathing the way I learnt when doing Tai Chi. I do this for my own patients: teach them deep, continuous breathing. A good majority of people do shallow breathing (using only the upper lobes of the lung, when using all of the lung lobes is necessary).

I was not permitted to lift my arms (while drain in situ); these were the only exercises:

- make a fist and release it
- to raise my forearms and lower them again
- to raise and lower my hands while my arms rested on a pillow

I was discharged on day two with drain in situ; my nephew Dan and his partner Ranya took me home and stayed the night. I had three huge bouquets of flowers to admire.

I was not able to do much around the house; they ensured that I had enough food. When I did small loads of washing, I would hang it on the clothes rack to dry.

I managed to get the help of the neighbour Neil across the street, who mowed the lawn, and his wife Bonnie washed my hair.

A niece Kristy and her partner Greg came to visit from the south side. She had phoned to say that she was at my door. She had not been to my home previously, so when I looked and saw her at the neighbour's house across the street, we just laughed.

The surgeon called the following week to see me back in surgery on 17 December. I was first on the morning list, at yet a different hospital; as it was so close to Christmas, getting a theatre was difficult. Axillary clearance was required before further spreading occurred. During this time of year, people are trying to go on leave for the festive season, and private hospitals tend to reduce staff for that very reason. Hence, I got to have a scenic tour of hospitals of a sort. I did not mind at all; I just wanted to be free of cancer. Yes, my anxiety levels rose; that was natural. I was only human, after all. I meditated regularly in an attempt to keep my fears at bay.

Dream 4 (Lesson 7)

I had thrown the evil seducer from the previous dream into a massive cooking pot. He had accepted his fate. Succumbed, he was stewing away. I was shocked to see three people come to quickly take strips of flesh from him for themselves. They called out, "Wait, wait, I need some of that." He looked ever so ghastly and wretched, especially with all the roots visible and exposed, yet they were convinced that they needed a portion.

I thought, Why would anyone want a part of that evil-looking wretch? They must be crazy.

It was now quite obvious that I would recover fully, going by this dream. I couldn't help but wonder who would want such a dreadful disease.

Second Surgery

On the morning of 17 December, I was once again up at 04.30.

I fed Puss, showered, and had myself ready in time for Mike to take me to hospital for the next part of the surgery: the axillary clearance.

I was absolutely terrified and quite jittery.

> *Life isn't about waiting for the storm to pass,*
> *it's about learning to dance in the rain.*
>
> *Vivian Greene (1904 – 2003)*

I was asked the usual questions when one of the staff noticed that I had a drain in situ.

To settle my nerves, I played a joke on them by saying (with a straight face), "Yes, I did an audit on the previous hospital and now I'm doing one here."

Their eyes widened and chins dropped.

I laughed and laughed, saying, "I'm only joking—honest."

I'm sure I wet myself with fear.

A fellow named Michael had checked me into theatre; I caught a glimpse of him on the way out and thanked him.

I thought to myself, *Archangel Michael is here watching over me.*

Result

A further nine nodes were removed (one was affected), making a total of fifteen, with four affected.

The following day, one of my colleagues Ula, came to visit. She gave me a gift in the form of a small book titled *This Too Shall Pass.*

We chattered for some time. I showed her my wound. She was happy that I looked and sounded well. We hugged before she left, then I sat and read the book. I felt so inspired by the book and knew I had to get back to as normal a routine as possible.

First, I had to change the mindset of my family, whose thoughts were rested on our youngest sister Margaret, who had passed away. I also had to get everyone else connected to me in any way to thinking happy, positive thoughts. Family and friends were openly saying things in a negative nature which sapped the positive energy from me. This affected me greatly, action had to be taken for my health and well-being. I need positive, happy thoughts to surround me thus, to aide my recovery.

The breast care nurse gave me several booklets for myself, family, and friends to go through. I flicked through one on relaxation. As I read the headings, it became apparent that the pages had a lot of empty space on them.

I was inspired to fill these spaces with positive sayings and famous words of famous people. These came from the little book Ula had given me.

I wrote all evening. I wondered if I could have more copies of this relaxation book. I ended up with a dozen. Over the weeks ahead, I repeated the same through all copies and gave them to family, friends, and a few people who I felt were in need. This proved to be excellent therapy.

Once again, on day two, I was discharged with drain in situ; Maree took me home.

My surgeon had booked me for two scans on 22 December: one of my skeleton—one millilitre of iodine is injected into the vein, then scanning takes place after waiting until it filters through the body. The other scan looked at all my soft tissue, which could only take place after drinking one litre of radioactive iodine drink and waiting until it filtered through my body. This was to search for secondary cancers.

It would take the best part of the day, approximately six to eight hours.

Bills had come from all directions. Emergency sickness funds were unavailable until four months form my superfund. Instead, I set up a "transition to retirement" package, receiving two lump sums a year; this proved the best option to pay for the bills.

Not sure how I was going to survive, I confided in my GP, who gave me a referral to St. Johns Ambulance to transport me to and from the hospital (for the scans) for a small fee, as I had no one available to take me and cash already being an issue.

I decided to ask my surgeon to give me a sickness certificate, allowing me to do light duties at work. This was the only way I could continue paying my mortgage and my bills and simply survive. She was very concerned about my return to work, especially in my line of work, but I assured her that I would be sensible.

Further Diagnostic Tests

After booking in at the radiology lab, I was first taken in to have the injection, then I drank the litre and waited more than an hour. I continued to wait until it had sufficiently filtered through my body. The whole skeleton scan was done first, then the whole body tissue.

On arriving home from the scans, my third brother Andrew and his wife Maria had arrived; they left two days earlier and had driven over fifteen hundred kilometres to get here. They had planned their journey some time before, as their daughter Nancy, at the Gold Coast was getting close to having her first baby, plus it was Christmas. They spent two nights with me.

The following day, 23 December, Andrew took me to the surgeon to get the results of the scans. She also wanted to see how much swelling I had and whether she would aspirate any fluid out with a needle or not. I'm so glad that she chose not to, as I believe it to be quite painful.

The surgeon also sent a referral to have genetic testing, due to my family history and also due to the fact that I have European Jewish blood—apparently a predominant factor—on my mother's side.

After I left her room, I noticed Andrew where he sat in the waiting room, he was crying; tears were streaming down his face.

I looked at him and said, "There's no need or time for tears."

Then I clicked my heels together and skipped out, singing, "It's a Merry, Merry Christmas!"

Results

Andrew laughed and cried as I informed him that the results were clear. There was a small cyst on the ovary, which they want removed at some point, but it was not urgent, as it was only a cyst. It had to go, as my sister Margaret had died of ovarian cancer; I had a strong a family history. Plus once one enters menopause, cysts have a habit of changing.

We headed a few floors down to the medical oncologist. For the life of me, I could not understand the need for chemo or radiation; my mind was still in denial. I guess I knew that I would be very ill, and I was trying to avoid it at all costs.

Besides, I felt I was already healed. I felt so well; why spoil it by giving chemo?

I pleaded my case, as I remembered how ill Margaret used to be, but he was having none of that; he knew what had to be done, as all the test results had been so damming.

In the end, I just wanted to be able to celebrate Christmas and New Year. He booked chemo to start 8 January 2016.

I had the same oncologist that my sister Margaret had; it was a relief, as she had trusted him 100 percent.

The garden and house now looked unloved; I knew that I wouldn't be able to take care of the property in years to come. After mowing the lawn and vacuuming the house and doing the washing, Andrew and Maria left for the Gold Coast on Christmas Eve.

Mike took me to Maree's place Christmas Day. We had a wonderful day and evening; looking at the Christmas lights in the street before heading home. My grandson, Xander (then aged four) had kept stroking my arm throughout the day. This amused me; as a general rule, he's quite boisterous.

As I was unable to lift my arms, Maree washed my hair in the shower. She seemed to look queasy at the sight of my wound; I expect the drain coming out from my chest didn't help.

On Boxing Day, Mike took me to the hospital to have the drain removed; what a relief. I could now move my arms, even though movement was limited due to contracted muscles. It was fantastic to be able to wash my own hair.

Trust life ...
life catches up with us and teaches us to love and forgive each other.

Judy Collins (1939–)

Nurses have to teach patients how to care for themselves. Even though I am a nurse, the breast care nurses diligently went through the process of refreshing my memory. When lymph nodes are removed, the body compensates by "rerouting" the lymph fluid through other lymph vessels in the area.

However, this system is not efficient. If these vessels are overloaded, lymph fluid may pool in the tissues, causing the swelling known as lymphedema.

Triggers of lymphedema include infections in the arm, being overweight, overheating the arm, injuries to the arm, carrying/holding heavy things, restricting circulation to upper body and arm, and travelling long distances.

Risks can be reduced by taking good care of skin, keeping active, using luggage on wheels, wearing a shoulder bag on the unaffected arm, exercising the arm while travelling, taking regular walks, and wearing a compression sleeve for long trips.

Movement and exercise are essential. Massage, even light tapping on the areas of lymphatic tissue, can stimulate circulation and encourage removal of built-up fluid. Brushing the skin stimulates the lymph system to eliminate waste more effectively. Drinking pure water helps to flush toxins and wastes from your system.

Post-Surgery

First Short Drive

Now permitted to drive short distances, I drove to the hospital on Dec.30 for a pelvic ultra sound. My sister Margaret had died from ovarian cancer, also during menopause cysts have a habit of changing more-so. While driving, I had reversed into a post, putting a small dent on the bumper. My arm was weaker than I had realised.

On New Year's Day, Mike took me for an appointment with the surgeon. She checked for swelling and lymphedema, she seemed pleased with my progress. She gave me my clearance to return to work on light duties.

The physio said to do arm exercises four times a day, every day. I also had to massage my arm and chest wall four times a day, to guide the lymph fluid away. This was not only very tiring but also quite painful; I had to hold my arms up in the air to do it. It is a depressing feeling knowing that this will have to continue for a few years. I knew it would be worth it in the end.

The next day, I took a train to the Gold Coast for my Nancy's baby shower. It was a nice relaxing day. But on the drive home with Nancy's in-laws, my seat belt was painful to wear across my chest; I had to tuck it under my arm and wear it across my abdomen.

On 5 January, I took myself to have my pre-chemo echo (ultrasound of the heart). Driving was fine but I parked so that I didn't have to reverse. I spent the day at Maree's place the next day for my granddaughter Mae's birthday.

The heads of the hospital were happy to accommodate me for my return to work on light duties. Making light of my condition, I said that I lost a mammary gland and that I didn't wish to lose my memory.

Back to Work

My first day back, I worked a shift in Day Surgery. It was an extremely busy day; I had not worked there before and so didn't know the layout or routine.

It was great, though, as I felt useful again—at last.

My spirit soared.

What a relief, knowing now that my home would not be repossessed. I had thought that I might end up on the street.

Not knowing how many shifts I would get, I went and asked my bank to put my mortgage payments on hold for a couple of months. I was ahead with payments, but not too far ahead.

After work one day, I went for a surgical review on my way home. The doctor was happy with the wound and my arm, especially how I presented after a busy shift at work.

Some work colleagues (Leonie, Deb, Kate, Anne) and friends (Michelle, Kim, Chris) had given gifts wishing me well; I appreciated this very much.

Recovery is a process, not an event.

Anne Wilson Schaef (DOB 1934)

The day of my treatment (IV Chemo) was imminent, and anxiety tried to take over. Somehow, I managed to have everyone believe that I was totally calm about everything. What I was doing was trying to stay calm so that everyone would stay positive with me, for me. In my mind, this was my top priority right now.

When making up your mind about something, your energy changes. Intention is the collection of energy. This energy is then focused, and inspired action follows. The benefits reach far into every aspect of life. It can be life changing.

Once again, the nursing staff diligently informed me on what to expect and what to do in case of emergency.

I was to let staff know if the injection site became red or painful, or if I had a rash, itching, a fever, shivers, dizziness, or breathlessness.

At home, I was to take medications as prescribed, take regular mouth care for forty-eight hours post-treatment, drink eight to ten glasses of fluid, empty my bladder often, go to nearest hospital if I experienced shortness of breath, a temperature over 38°C, continuous vomiting, or chills.

I could expect these side effects: nausea and vomiting, red-coloured urine, change in sense of smell and taste, increased risk of infection, low platelets, diarrhoea or constipation, sensitive skin, a sore mouth, tiredness, and hair loss.

Also possible but less likely to occur were poor concentration, nail damage, and heart changes.

Things to avoid:

- raw food drink; unwashed fruit/vegetables
- green tea
- aspirin, ibuprofen and other anti-inflammatories
- omega-3 and similar oils

I should maintain a healthy diet, being mindful that some foods can put one at risk, such as raw foods, raw drinks, and unwashed fruit/vegetables.

The use of plastic utensils when eating; helps prevent a metallic taste in the mouth.

Mouthwash: use ½ teaspoon salt in a glass warm water or 1 teaspoon baking soda in a glass warm water.

Toothpaste has a very metallic taste; mouthwash is the better choice.

First Chemo (IV)

I was in the Oncology Unit by 8.00 on 8 January to receive my first dose of chemo to be given "Intra Venous". It began with a cannula—in my right hand, as my left hand could no longer be used for tests due to lymphedema—and then blood tests. After the results were read, I was given a pre-med antiemetic, and the chemo followed.

I had a headache after the pre-med started. I had to go to the toilet while it was still running in via drip. I was queasy and unsteady.

Even though I had breakfast, the staff said that I must be dry; they gave me drinks and sandwiches, saying to eat and drink what I could, and I did enjoy them, then I noticed a change in my taste. Sadly, my headache did not improve. The nurses told me to drink more, as it was important to do so with the effect of the chemo.

On arriving home after the treatment, I initially felt no worse. I kept my fluids up. As the day progressed, I became weak and very unsteady. I started to become restless, not knowing whether to lay down, stand, or sit. My temperature was 37°C.

I continued to eat and drink as often as I could. I was in and out of bed constantly—I was so very restless. By 2 a.m., my headache had become a migraine. I was also dizzy. My heart was racing and chest cramping.

I boiled some eggs to have with a cup of tea. It seemed forever before it was morning.

I took my antiemetics when due, as in the past, I had become giddy and that would lead to vomiting. As I was having trouble concentrating, I used a note pad to record the time I took my medications, along with their names, to ensure I didn't over (or) under-dose.

Regardless, I started to regurgitate; drinking ginger ale or iced tea helped. I lost skin in my mouth and tongue and down my throat, making me extremely nauseated. The skin peeled like the fine membrane between an egg shell and a boiled egg. It would grow back and peel again and again.

At times, I dry-retched to the point of tears flowing down my face, or else I would simply vomit. The taste was so very vile. I could swear I could taste the chemo.

My mouth was so raw that I had to be very careful not to eat crackers or anything else hard and crunchy, as my mouth would bleed. Chewing crackers or toast felt like gravel and broken glass. I had to settle my stomach another way; I could tolerate soft white bread.

My eyes were constantly weeping, yet I knew I wasn't crying (I was too sick to cry). The discharge was sticky and gluggy; I washed my eyes regularly.

If that wasn't enough, I had a vaginal discharge causing ulceration in the perineal region; this made it hurt to go to the toilet. (I bathed the area in salty water regularly until healed.)

Alex brought the children for a visit while he did the lawn for me. It was a lovely distraction. By the end of the second week, about 90 percent of my hair had fallen out from all over my body.

My scalp and head hurt; they felt as though I had been beaten. My hair fell out in clumps, and then the pain eased.

At home and out shopping, I wore a small straw hat. I purchased some fabric to make scarves, which I did before returning to work.

The oncologist phoned on 12 January. On informing him of my side effects, he told me that he would add reflux medication to my pre-med process.

I filled out some forms from Genetic Health and returned them as instructed. As there was a long waiting list, I was told it could take some months before they get back to me.

I worked on 15, 16, and 17 January. I felt car sick in transit, but that settled once I focused on what had to be done during the shift. I was now back on my own ward, a very busy orthopaedic ward, but I was still on light duties. It was very tiring and relentless, but I was so happy to be there.

A colleague, Carol welcomed me with a big hug, saying how well I looked, considering what I had been through. I thanked her, telling her that it was like going to hell and back.

One day, while attending a patient, my scarf had fallen off, so I decided to make something better. I managed to get a few operating theatre hats, pulling one apart to use as a pattern. I made three fabric hats, which were easier to wear than scarves.

I had a radiation therapy appointment on 21 January. To save money on car parking fees, I drove partway and then took the bus.

I was a mental wreck; I had no desire to suffer any more treatment. In my mind, I was saying, "Don't they think I've been through enough already? Do they know how it feels? Have they actually had treatment themselves? I'm getting pushed from one to the other like an object."

My mind was having no part of this.

Finally, my name was called. The radiation oncologist was very calm and caring. She looked deep into my eyes and told me that radiation and chemo treatments are to "mop up" any cells still lurking. I cried, sobbing deep within. I hugged her and thanked her for the explanation.

Being at the radiation clinic was also a reality check for me in another way, seeing how ill other people were. It had been a long time since I had worked in a public hospital. Some patients' burns looked so very painful.

I worked on 22, 23, 25, and 28 January. The head surgeon came and spoke to me, asking how I was coping with being at work. I explained I had a psychological need to be there due to family history and for my emotional and financial welfare; he agreed.

I attempted to do some embroidery. It made me feel very depressed, and besides, I was not feeling up to doing it. I could not settle into the adult colouring books, either.

You tend to dwell on negativity while doing such mundane tasks in this state. I needed to be busy and focused, which was why going to work was so good.

> *There is nothing to be gained by wishing you were someplace else or waiting for a better situation.*
> *You see where you are, and you do what you can with that.*
>
> *Jacob K. Javits (1904–1986)*

Second Chemo

On 29 January, I had my second dose of chemo, this time in the afternoon. Knowing what the next week would bring, I went reluctantly to the oncology unit; tears were in my eyes as I started to backpedal. The nurse took my hand. I was given a different pre-med and something for reflux to help with the mouth ulcers.

I was also given a sedative, which meant that I stayed in hospital for the weekend (it took this long for the sedative to wear off).

After my drip was removed prior to discharge, a small ulcer had developed under the cannula; I had to be very careful not to get it wet.

I spent the day at Maree's, where I slept for a few hours.

I had taken the regular antiemetic but was still unable to eat much; I had meal-replacement drinks every now and then.

Initially, for the first four days I had constipation which was to exacerbate the nausea, then suddenly diarrhoea to the extreme, until nil but mucus came away. With a fine line between the two, I had to balance the medications, not over medicate or under medicate. The reflux medication helped a little; my mouth, tongue, and throat still peeled, just not so severe (still had nausea, though).

I also had a great deal of discomfort from the PV discharge, which burned the perineal area.

The skin on my body also peeled, especially my feet. My muscles and bones ached. Once the nausea settled, I was still unable to eat very much. Some foods actually caused more nausea, like onions, peas, and corn. I was still unable to eat dry, hard, or crisp foods due to ulcers. Other foods caused diarrhoea, so I had to be mindful to only eat these in moderation. Bonox (a beef broth which is purchased as a concentrate) was a good staple standby as a hot drink. Ice blocks or "icy poles" were an excellent relief for my mouth.

I had regular visits to the physiotherapist, who massaged the lymphedema to help it drain away. She also went through a regime of exercises that assisted in fluid movement. This helped me get movement and strength back, little by little.

During the summer, I wore a straw hat instead of a scarf in the home and out shopping. The suggestion of a wig in this heat made me cringe. Not only that, the chemo makes you feel hot (especially your head), and this leads to nausea. As my hair thinned more and more, hats would turn or spin on my head. I had woolly hats, but these were far too hot in this heat, so off I went to get some fabric to make a beret.

I worked on 5 to 8 February; once again, focusing on the job at hand helped me to forget my troubles.

I have this motto:

"Act well,
feel well,
be well."
Well, it worked a lot of the time.

Pus, having seen me visit the neighbour, often went next door, looking for me, when I was at work.

One day while I was getting my car serviced, I rang my sister Jeanette. I didn't want to be alone for treatment any longer. I felt traumatised and was an emotional wreck, knowing the hellish effects I could expect from each chemo treatment. I knew how I would feel, and this left me depressed and crying. I wondered if I could continue with it. It was very tempting to leave it all up to Mother Nature.

Jeanette immediately told me that she could come and stay with me for a few weeks; she arranged to arrive by train the day before my next chemo treatment.

I tried to remain busy so that my anxiety levels were at a minimum until she arrived.

On 11 February, Mike left for a European holiday with a friend. This made me both happy and a little sad. He would be in Europe for his birthday, and it was his first time leaving the country. I was excited for him and half-wished I could go too. I so wanted to run away from the treatment (and myself—especially myself). I looked forward to his return.

I worked from 12 to 15 February; emotionally, I was on top of everything at the moment. I knew that Jeanette was on her way from far north Queensland – more than 1500 kilometres away.

I always felt tired, with aching bones and muscles. I felt like I may break into pieces; my bones and whole body made cracking noises as I walked.

The physio gave me a massage to loosen all my tight muscles (they were so tight, like ropes under my skin being visible as they had contracted.) This was really very painful, but I knew it had to happen in order to have full movement of my shoulder and arm. I was shown more exercises to assist with my strength and range of movement—for radiation, I needed to be able to hold my arms above my head for half an hour while laying still.

I spent the day with Maree's family.

I had been waiting on the platform as Jeanette's train pulled in, all the while on the lookout for her. To my dismay, she walked right past me. I followed her and then tapped her on the shoulder. She had been focused on collecting her luggage while chatting to the other passengers she had travelled with.

Not long after getting home from the train, a woman came to fit my prosthesis and bra. I had chosen not to have an implant. The prosthesis was a lot heavier than it looked.

Third Chemo

On 19 February, Jeanette helped me face the third chemo. It was another week of hell. Being extremely attentive, Jeanette did all she could to relieve my woes for the duration of her stay.

Puss kept us amused with her antics, enjoying the toys I had given her. She also took to laying on her back with her belly fully exposed. For fun, I 'nick-named' her Jezebel.

My nephew Dan and his family came to visit, even though I wasn't much company. It was great having them visit. Having people around me helped me forget the effects of chemo somewhat. Not only that, I wanted them to keep happy thoughts in their mind.

In February, NBN (National Broadband Network) which is being installed across the nation was installed; I loved having any distraction while feeling lousy.

On 23 February, the prosthesis and bras arrived; I almost had to be a contortionist, tying myself in knots to get it on and off. As I was unable to reach behind my back, I decided to try another way of doing the bra: hook it together in the front then put the prosthesis in after bringing it to the front, then put the straps up. To take it off: pull the straps down, remove prosthesis, turn it so it hooks at the front, and undo.

I wasn't sure that I would be bothering too much with prosthesis (so heavy) and bra so uncomfortable, unless I went out or to work.

On 26 February, I went to work, starting to feel some sort of normality again since last chemo.

I could only tolerate small amounts of a very bland diet, bland soups, and bonox. Meal-replacement drinks were a great alternative, as were ice blocks.

On 27 February, Maree took me to the theatre, where we watched a traditional Chinese song and dance performance called *Shen Yun*. It was very spiritual, magical, and beautiful. I loved it so much.

Jeanette spent the day with her sons Gordon and Fred and grandchildren Min, Bea and Seb while we were at the show. My niece Jean in Toowoomba was unable to come visit her mother due to having shingles, which is not only contagious but can put someone on chemo into organ failure (in a worst-case scenario).

I worked the next two days, still feeling very calmed and charmed after having been to the show.

One of the managers, Madeline gave me some silk scarves, so I decided to wear one to work; to my embarrassment, it fell off in front of a patient. She was accepting of me as to how I was.

I spent the day with Maree's family on 2 March. Mike was back from his European holiday. As his lease had expired, I asked him to move in. He started bringing car loads of his things over each day after work.

I worked on 4 and 5 March, feeling so much better about everything while Jeanette was staying with me.

One of the surgeons asked why I started wearing scarves at work. When I told him, he was shocked to hear I had had chemo, saying that I looked too well. All I could say to that is that the angels really took care of me in every way.

On 6 March, we went to the 'Fun Run' which is held every year to raise money for breast cancer research. My colleagues Sonja, Elanore and Ashley entered, running in honour of me with the team name "Who Needs Twin Peaks?"

I had thought to walk, but my legs would not cooperate, so we all met for breakfast afterwards. Jeanette joined her sons Gordon and Fred and grandchildren Min, Bea and Seb while I was with my colleagues.

On 7 March, I worked; I was totally bald now, eyebrows and eyelashes included. My toenails were lifting, making it uncomfortable to wear shoes.

Puss often waited for me on the footpath. She would run inside and wait while I put the car in the garage.

On the morning of 9 March, my cousin Frederick, his wife Chris, and his ninety-four-year-old mother (my Aunt Elsie) came to visit. Aunt Elsie is a throat cancer survivor. After answering all their questions about my health, we had a lovely morning with loads of talking and laughter.

I had another physio appointment for exercising and massage; it gave my tight, painful muscles some needed relief. My bones creaked and cracked when I walked or moved. I felt fragile, as though I was going to snap into pieces.

Fourth Chemo

My fourth chemo was on 11 March; Jeanette went with me (they also changed drugs that day). I was the first patient in the unit for the day, all going to plan, starting with cannula and blood tests. With blood tests normal, I went through the pre-med process. Then, a few minutes after the drug commenced, I started to feel squashed (as if someone was sitting right on top of me), and I struggled to breathe. I actually thought I was going to die right there and then.

The drip was turned off, and one drug after the other was injected. I fell asleep after what seemed like a long time. Eventually, I recovered and was discharged home.

I was quite shaken from the whole experience. Jeanette was a mess.

Mike had now fully moved in, every room was quite cramped, but that was the least of my troubles. My niece Bride and her family arrived for the day from Beaudesert to visit her mother. This was a great distraction.

With Jeanette's train due to leave in the afternoon, her daughter-in-law Jade came with Seb, the youngest of her grandsons. We said our farewells, and they left for the station for her journey to Charters Towers. Her presence was missed in the coming weeks. Puss also noted her absence.

On 16 March, I spoke to the doctor, who informed me that I would be put back on the other drugs, as this had been a long-proven treatment. A picc line—a tube going through the blood vessel from the upper arm to the heart—would be inserted before the treatment started. As I was with my daughter for the day, I was able to inform her immediately.

> *A kind word to one in trouble is often like a switch in a railroad track …*
> *An inch between a wreck and smooth sailing.*
>
> *Henry Ward Beecher (1813–1887)*

Puss was now starting to sit on my lap for short periods.

I worked from 18 to 21 March; it was an excellent distraction for my woes. I drank meal-replacement drinks being one of the only thing I could tolerate. I asked a few of my colleagues, Anita, Kate, Leonie and Adrika if any of them would be able to come along with me for future treatments. They would be happy to oblige, provided they were not rostered on duty. Kate was free and willing to come with me for my next treatment.

Puss seemed much more relaxed and was getting accustomed to my comings and goings. She finally seems to realize that she is welcome in her new home.

Fifth Chemo and Picc Insertion

On 22 March, my colleague Kate took me to treatment. First, I had to go down to the radiology lab for the insertion of the picc line. This was due to the fact that my veins were now collapsed from the chemo. Kate stayed with me, and I relaxed as we conversed over all sorts of topics. The blood tests were followed by the pre-med process and then the treatment.

It's a good thing to have all the props pulled out from under us occasionally. It gives us some sense of what is rock under our feet and what is sand.

Madeleine L'Engle (1918–2007)

I returned the following morning to have a change of dressing on the picc line. I was starting to feel a bit woozy from the treatment.

On the morning of 26 March, while having breakfast, a few drops of blood fell to the floor from the picc site.

Mike was present at the time; I said to him, "Feel like driving me to the hospital?"

I phoned the hospital to inform them that I was on my way. On arrival, I was put onto a bed with my arm elevated and iced. Half an hour later, they changed the dressing, and I was on my way home, as all was well.

The physio did not want to see me while the picc line in place (it seems I had overdone it with exercises.) I was just to do gentle movements and gentle stretches so that my muscles didn't contract any further.

Now taking extra care with both arms. My muscles pulled across my chest and under my arm. They would contract and get tight, being visible under the skin; it looked like a thick rope. This was all very, very painful, giving me the feeling of being restrained.

I also felt as though something was wedged under my arm from the back. This fluid from the lymphedema went from the elbow up, across my shoulder, and down my chest wall. If I did too much, the fluid went right down my arm into my fingers. Occasionally, I would be so distressed from this that I would simply cry to release.

I worked on 28 March; it was good to be there in the company of others and with something else to focus on; it was also good to get home afterwards, being so exhausted.

A colleague Lynn who had a mastectomy and clearance fourteen years ago informed me that I would get some tattoos for radiation. She has three dot-sized tattoos that were used as markers (which are used with the lights that lined the patient up for positioning).

I spoke to my cousin Jane, who had been through this ten years ago; she also has three dot-sized tattoos, for the same reason.

To save money on the car park at the hospital, I drove as far as a convenient free car park two suburbs from the hospital. From there, I took the bus to the hospital.

As I had heard horror stories about radiation therapy, I was quite anxious. The consultant, a rather pleasant woman, soon had me feeling more at ease. I spent the following day with Maree and family. It was a long tiresome day, but it was good having company.

I took Mike to the airport on 31 March, as he was to be best man at a mate's wedding the following day.

I needed the picc dressing done, and I called in at the oncology unit before going to Maree's place.

My eldest granddaughter Leigh, who was ten years old, would be staying me the next few days. She cried as she expressed her fears about whether she would have to go through what I was going through. I reassured her and comforted her.

She played my singing bowls and sat with my crystals as we talked. We had an enjoyable few days together playing games, shopping, and exploring.

Alex and Xander came to do a few jobs in the garden, and then they all went home together.

I worked on 4 April; my colleague Anne puts together a wonderful Easter raffle each year; much to my surprise, they presented me with the proceeds.

On 5 April, my youngest brother Duncan, his wife Lynette, and group of friends came for the day. We had a fabulous time catching up during a hearty lunch. There was a lot to laugh about, and we had an enjoyable visit. My heart was singing.

Preparations for Radiation

I had an appointment at the radiation clinic on 6 April; I took my car to the free car park and then rode by bus the remainder of the way.

At the clinic, I first spoke with a fellow who asked a load of questions and then told me a little of what to expect. He gave me an appointment for 23 May and explained that treatment would be every day, Monday to Friday, until 27 June. He also informed me that the appointment would last at least twenty minutes each day.

I returned to the waiting room until being called to have a mould made of my shape; this was done on a thing like a bean bag; they removed the air to keep it in the exact shape, now being solid. After the mould was made, I returned to the waiting room until the consultant arrived. On her return, she marked the areas on my skin where I would be treated, a gelatine mould was made of this marked area. My arms ached, having had to hold them above my head for ever so long.

Next, the tattoos, five in total, due to the area to be treated: two on each side of my chest wall, toward the rear (and below) each armpit (about eleven centimetres apart), and one in the centre of my chest, over the sternum.

One of my friends joked that I needed leathers now that I had tattoos.

A repeat cardiac echo was done on 7 April, to ensure that were no changes.

My niece Joan had a precautionary bowel resection done the same day; it turned out to be cancer of the appendix.

I constantly felt tired, with aching bones and muscles; my big toenails also hurt, as they were lifting off and rubbing on my shoes. I tried different shoes in an attempt to relieve the pressure.

Sixth Chemo (Attempt 1)

On 8 April, another of my colleagues, Leonie came along with me for the chemo treatment. She really gave me the courage required to get me through this. However, the blood test showed my white cell count was too low to go ahead; treatment would have to wait a few more days.

It was great having her with me as I needed to talk about it. In a way, I was glad the treatment was postponed, but in another way, I just wanted it over.

My mind was a blank, so she Googled what to take to build up white cells. We called in at the chemist on the way home to get the vitamins necessary to support my immune system.

My niece, Nancy and her new baby Grace were coming from the Gold Coast the next day, so I made a conscious effort to do some housework for the first time since before the surgery. Just looking at food made me queasy, so I was eating poorly.

The next day Nancy and her family came. I managed to get my share of cuddles with Grace while we took some family photos.

Sixth Chemo (Attempt 2)

The following day, my young colleague Leonie attended chemo with me again. She was such a treasure, making the process that much more bearable, especially knowing I would be so ill again.

I spent the following day relaxing with Maree. I essentially lazed around; my toes hurt with the nails lifting.

Two days later, I went to the oncology unit for the picc dressing. I still required constant, regular antiemetics for the nausea.

I worked on 16 to 18 April; one of my patients was a Brother (educator at a Catholic school) he and another Brother and two Nuns (Catholic Sisters) were visiting him. They were quite intrigued as to why I wore my scarf.

When I explained that I was being treated for breast cancer, they were stunned. One of the Nuns revealed that she had been treated for it some years earlier. She felt that I had a strength more than she. I told them that I wasn't sure about that, but my belief system and prayers were my strength. The angels really carried me every inch of the way.

I returned to the unit on 21 April to change the picc dressing.

I worked from 22 to 25 April; I also had a flu vaccination.

I spent the day at Maree's place on 27 April.

Friends, Enester and Franco from Innisfail came to visit the next day. It was a great time catching up on news of each other over a light hearted lunch.

Seventh Chemo

I had my last chemo on 29 April. Thank God at last; I thanked God also that my young colleague Leonie was able to be with me again. What a relief.

My treatment went ahead even though my white cell count was low again; I sighed a sigh of relief.

Leonie and I chatting all the while; we rarely got the chance to talk at work.

Once the chemo was complete, the picc line was removed. I faced another week of being ill but for the last time.

I thanked God that the Intra Venous Chemo was finally complete. It had been an emotional roller coaster, plus a turmoil of hellish struggles.

I finally got around to making my beret.

When you have gone so far that you can't manage one more step, then you've gone just half the distance that you're capable of.

Greenland Proverb

On 5 May, my sister Irene, niece Clair and her father Francis from Mackay spent the night in Brisbane before flying to New Zealand the following morning.

I met them at their hotel for dinner but was too nauseated to eat, so I just had a small serving of rice.

I worked the next three days, called in at my Maree's on the way to work to give Xander his birthday present.

I received two beautiful bouquets of flowers for Mother's Day; I loved nature's gifts.

I went to the physio on 10 May and had the usual exercises and lymph massage. The muscles tight and contracted, she had a lot of work to do on me.

My house and garden were neglected, as I spent all my strength and energy at work. I did manage to give the floor a rough sweep, though.

I was unable to tolerate food at all, so I tended to pick at small amounts when I did. I spent the day with Maree on 11 May. I worked on 13 and 14 May, feeling very tired.

Many staff members from other departments came to my ward, curious about my wearing a scarf. They asked if I was working between the theatre and the ward, and they were shocked to learn I was having treatment.

They all said how well I looked.

Thank you, thank you, thank you, angels!

On 15 May, Dan and Ranya came over with Irene. She had been with them for a few days after having been in New Zealand.

Puss often brought us gifts from outside in the form of lizards, crickets, and worms. As they were still alive, we scooped them up and put them back outside, much to the disappointment of Pus.

On 16 May, Irene came to work with me, where she met up with an old school friend in the city. The next day, I took her to the Gold Coast to meet our newest great-niece, Grace. We all enjoyed lunch at the Surf Club and then called in to see my Maree and family on our way home.

The next day, she wanted to go shoe shopping, so we went to the mall. While there, we had lunch at the Vietnamese restaurant. Still eating poorly, I had a small bowl of rice.

On 19 May, we went to visit Aunt Elsie (Mum's sister) she's ninety-four. She and their older brother Andrew, had both been treated for cancer. She loved having visitors, and we found plenty to talk about.

Irene returned to Mackay on 20 May; I dropped her at the airport on my way to work. I also worked the next day. As my anxiety levels were now quite elevated in anticipation of the radiation, I took the following day off.

With the cooler weather approaching, I took my slippers out to wear. When Puss saw them, she jumped in the air with fright and ran off. I had not given any thought to the fact that the front of my slipper was made to look like a ladybug with a smiley face.

During the night, I woke and saw Pus with her claws in the face of one of the slippers; she had pulled it to the door of my bedroom. She may have towed the other one off also, had I not decided to put them out of sight.

A few days later, she was no longer afraid of my slippers, though she still claws them from time to time.

The physio that I had been seeing moved on, so I managed to get a few sessions in at the hospital.

Healing is simply attempting to do more of those things that bring joy and fewer of those things that bring pain.

Dr. O. Carl Simonton (1942–2009)

The radiation nurses were on the ball and diligently told me all the dos and don'ts.

I was advised that skin changes are different for each person depending on what part of your body is being treated, amount of radiation given, possible medications due at same time, and whether you have diabetes or other illnesses.

I will get variations of skin changes may include colour (pink or bright red); feeling warm to touch; dry, itchy, flaky, or sensitive skin; pain or swelling, and blisters or weeping.

These changes usually begin ten to fourteen days after treatment commences and may get worse as it continues. Changes can be at their worst a week or so after treatment finishes, then they usually improve and healing well by four to six weeks after radiation therapy finishes.

I was advised to contact the doctor/nurse or go to nearest emergency ward if my temperature exceeds 38°C or if I had severe pain, continued swelling, blistering, redness, bleeding, pus, sores, or moist skin.

I was informed to take particular care of my skin to clean with warm water and unscented soap, rinse well, pat skin dry, rather than rubbing. Also to take short, lukewarm or cool baths/showers if I preferred. A salt water bath was helpful for itchy skin. I must moisturise my skin from first day of treatment, using moisturiser at least twice daily. Keeping moisturiser in fridge proved to soothe the skin. I was not permitted to apply cleansers or moisturisers within two hours before treatment.

I used Sunlight laundry soap, as it's unscented.

These following moisturisers are available from the pharmacy, I tried them all.

- QV
- David Craig Sorbolene Cream
- Moo Goo Udder (unscented, free of petroleum and metals)

I was told to avoid using deodorants, talcum powder, perfumes, makeup, dressings and creams containing metals, petroleum, sunblock as it has an effect on treatment.

They said not to rub the skin or wear tight clothing. When outdoors, I must try to stay in the shade and wear a hat and loose-fitting cotton clothing.

I felt the need to go on retreat into the hills, somewhere, anywhere in nature to regain my composure, to recharge my batteries, and to get the wind back in my sails, if just for a day or two.

I was feeling unsafe; I couldn't find my zone of safety. Being spiritually lost, I was in a state of anxiety. I was having issues trying to relax—entering that place where the nervous system is relaxed so that I could go within to my inner peace.

In one way, I knew what I should do, but in another way, I was thinking that would be like willing myself to die (committing myself to spirit). I even wrote a poem to that effect; after reading it, I closed down. I was totally confused as when I read what I had written, it sounded different to what I had intended, but no way was I going to tell anyone that.

The poem was about going home; "Going Home" is either going within to meditate but also it is to die. I was having difficulty finding my inner peace. Regardless, I continued my daily rituals of prayer in stillness, not about to give up on myself. A lot of focus went into talking to myself to help me through the process.

Hold on; hold fast; hold out. Patience is genius.

Comte De Buffon
(1707 - 1788)

As time goes on, the exercises change for toning and strength. There were three strengths of stretch bands: light, moderate, and heavy.

Initially, I used the light band, starting with three or four stretches/pulls of each exercise, gradually building up to ten or twelve over a few weeks before progressing to the moderate strength.

To help with massage in difficult areas, the physio suggested I use a brush for the strokes/ stroking, and a tennis ball around the shoulder joint. The tennis ball was a big improvement in and around the axilla. I put the ball in a long sock and then dropped it over my shoulder. I then backed up to a wall and moved around, leaning into the wall and thus massaging the area.

I also have half-kilogram and one-kilogram weights to do curls and other exercises. Again, I started off with the half-kilogram weight and progressed slowly before changing to the one-kilogram weight. At times, I held both in one hand, making 1.5 kilogram. I don't do this too often (not yet, anyhow).

Tai chi breathing helps with bowel health, as in massaging the bowel (due to the deep breathing) for regularity. I enjoy the movement of Tai Chi as it is calming and relaxing once the steps are remembered.

One morning Puss was waiting at her plate for breakfast. I served her meal, but she looked at it and made a disgruntled sound. She went outside and returned with a small lizard, which she dropped in the plate. Well, the lizard took off, and she was hot on its trail. She returned about an hour later and ate her breakfast.

I do get amused watching her antics, though other times I cringe.

She uses several vocal sounds which obviously have different meanings.

It is great to have her to return home to. She wants to be wanted and loved just the same as any person.

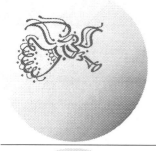

Radiation Therapy Treatment

There are twenty-five treatments, though some people have more. I was told by someone that people often get claustrophobic in the 'tunnel' (the radiation machine is called a tunnel by some as it is a large 'pipe-like' thing that patients are delivered into.) Some people needing some sedation to calm them. I also heard a lot of horror stories around radiation therapy. These things echoed in my head; with the treatment looming, my anxiety levels rose. I was in tears again.

One of the best safeguards of our hopes,
I have suggested,
is to be able to mark off the areas of hopelessness
and to acknowledge them,
to face them directly,
not with despair
but with the creative intent
of keeping them from polluting
all the areas of possibility.

William F. Lynch (1801–1865)

My first treatment was on 23 May. I could have sworn I felt something passing gently through my body, like a change in energy. I was a little dizzy after the treatment. The staff insisted that it was not possible to feel the treatment. The dizziness was put down to anxiety.

I had travelled by car and then bus to the hospital, so I took a few deep breaths and made my way to the bus station. After getting off the bus and making my way to the car, I felt fine and wondered what I had been so anxious about.

The following afternoon, I had another appointment. I was still anxious and tried to amuse myself in the 'tunnel' during treatment; the best I could do was sing and hum along with the music that the staff had playing. I also counted stickers and spots within view. I was unable to get to complete peace.

I continued to feel the treatment; it was an occasional stabbing pain.

I had taken some copies of shared learning from work to read while in the waiting room. This had two benefits: The first was to keep up with my CPD (Continuous Professional Development) points for work; second, it kept my mind from drifting into the negative side of life. All nurses must contribute a particular number of points to their learning each calendar year.

My appointment on 25 May was in the midmorning. This meant I had to be up early to go through all my rituals and get through the peak hour traffic. I then parked in the free parking to take the bus to the hospital.

I was very emotional, and the staff called the doctor. We talked through all my fears, and then I went back to the waiting room, ready for treatment.

I took off my clothes from the waist up (also removed my jewellery) and then put on a gown, which was pulled to one side after I was lying on the mould which was on the table then the chest mould was put in place. To be in perfect alignment (the same each time), the staff did a bit of pulling and pushing on my body. This is done using the five dot sized tattoos which were put on me to use as markers to be lined up with the lights. Alignment has to be exact to the millimetre so as not to cause damage to tissue they are trying to avoid. (example – the heart)

When they were all satisfied, a few buttons were pressed, and they left the room and watched from a monitor. The staff were able to hear if I needed to call them. The whole treatment sounded like a lot of rats or mice running around a wheel.

While I was seated in the waiting room, I heard staff read a meditation over the speaker to the woman in the treatment room. When her treatment was complete, she came past me, looking a bit rattled.

I thought to myself about what I had just seen and heard. I was glad I was not alone at being anxious. I really felt for her. Luckily, I was able to relax for my treatment; thank you, angels.

I must say, it was good to leave the hospital a little earlier. I spent the remainder of the day at Maree's place.

My next appointment was later the following day. I had a leisurely drive to the car park and then walked down to the bus station for the bus to the hospital.

I had been experiencing a constant cold chill across my shoulders due to sweating, even though the weather was cold. As it was a late appointment, I found myself in peak hour traffic on my return home. I am glad to say that I managed to stay calm for my appointment.

Peace does not mean to be in a place where there is no noise, trouble, or hard work. It means to be in the midst of all those things and still be calm in your heart.

Anon

My fifth treatment was a late-morning appointment on 27 May. I was struggling to read my shared learning for work. I seemed to be struggling with the fact that I was even there, having treatment.

While waiting in the changing room to go in, I noticed they kept me waiting a lot longer than usual. Finally, the doors opened, and another patient was escorted through. She was sobbing. The staff were explaining to her why they had to leave her in there so long: She had kept moving in the 'tunnel'. This meant they had to reposition her and line her up again, every time, and then restart the treatment. The poor lady was so distressed; I felt her pain.

I concentrated on not moving or coughing, as I had a throat irritation.

I was getting more and more stabbing pains; I also felt cold and yet, was sweating across my shoulders, I also had some difficulty swallowing.

The following day, I went to work. My heart was much lighter, as I simply focused on the job at hand.

I spent the next day catching up, doing laundry and not much else. My scalp looked all pimply, as though hair was trying to come through. There were still no further improvements with eating; I could only eat small amounts of bland food.

My sixth treatment was a late-morning appointment on 30 May. My skin was now lumpy with blisters and quite pink. I had tears in my eyes, not wanting to be there. I tried to meditate, plus I read every day from my spiritual books; I found solace in their contents.

I watched as a young woman came in with a little boy. As she checked in, the boy was very chatty, telling his mother to look as he recognised the staff members. I did not see them again until a week or so later.

Going in to the change room area just prior to my treatment, I noticed a big poster on the wall. It was covered with pictures of dogs, and between the dogs were thirty plain white squares, with a boy's name, Thomas across the top. I didn't initially think too much about the poster as it didn't alter over the first week. I would later come to realise that was soon to change. Apparently the staff, mother and Thomas had created this while teaching him to get on and off the table. The staff needed to know that Thomas would be able to cooperate as radiation had to be lined up exactly.

The following day, I had a late afternoon appointment and a doctor's appointment. My skin was now red and lumpy with blisters; it was also itchy, so the doctor ordered cortisone cream to use twice daily between the moisturisers. The doctor had been so calm and gentle, which made me more relaxed.

I noticed as I went through to the change room area that one of the white squares in the poster had been drawn on.

It took a long time to get home through the peak hour traffic.

Keep a green tree in your heart and perhaps the singing bird will come.

Chinese Proverb

My eighth treatment was a lunchtime appointment on 1 June.

I couldn't make myself read any of the shared learning from work, so I picked up a magazine. The puzzle had not been done, so I got my pen and went into action, thus keeping my mind busy.

The poster in the change-over area had another square scribbled on. I wished to meet this brave little soul. He gets to colour a square each day after his treatment.

Thursday saw me with an early-evening appointment, so I parked on the street behind the hospital. The treatment machine was playing up; it shut itself down twice and had to be restarted.

My stabbing pains persisted, and the sweat across my shoulders was now constant. I also seemed to cough a lot more these days, the radiation affecting my lungs.

My tenth treatment, on 3 June, was an evening appointment; I managed to do some housework before heading to the city. Again, I parked on the street behind the hospital.

I noticed that the poster now had five white squares scribbled on.

I had a big sneeze during my treatment; my feet lifted off the table. I was sure they would have to restart my treatment, but they didn't; what a relief.

I worked on 4 and 5 June. Though I focused on my work, I couldn't help but think of the poster with the dog pictures and white squares and the brave little boy, Thomas. I prayed that I would find a way to just relax into the treatment – Thomas was so brave.

I then realized my prayers had to change from asking the angels to simply be with me, to asking them to protect all healthy tissue.

At last, I was able to focus my energy with intention again (better late than never, as the saying goes), bringing myself inner peace.

It's better to light a candle than to curse the darkness.

Peter Benenson (1921 – 2005)

On 6 June, the radiation machine was being serviced, so I was able to do laundry and other chores. I also stayed focused on the machine only destroying unhealthy tissue, thus preserving healthy tissue. My perception of the whole affair had been totally unbalanced.

My eleventh treatment was the following afternoon; my skin was quite burnt. I drove to the free park and then took the bus to the hospital, feeling much more relaxed now with my healthier prayers.

Young Child: A Massive Inspiration

The following day, I had an early appointment, so I was up very early to get through traffic. After my treatment, while changing, I heard voices of a mother and child (was this Thomas.) I pulled back the curtain to see little Thomas and his mother. I sat in the change room with the curtain back, watching them go into the treatment room. As I sat and waited, a multitude of things went through my mind. He walked in fearlessly while holding his mother's hand. I felt shame, as I had been stricken with anxiety for so long.

As his mother started singing the ABC song, the tears came into my eyes. This little boy had gone in happily, with no fuss or bother. I had been acting up and now felt somewhat ashamed.

If this little guy could do it, I sure had to. He was such an inspiration to me.

I was with Maree the remainder of the day. I told her about Thomas and his mother. With my new lease on life, I was at peace and relaxed, now able to face treatment.

On 9 June, I had a lunchtime appointment. Duncan and his Lynette were in Brisbane for the caravan and camping show; I was to meet them after my treatment. Because of this, I parked in the hospital car park ($25 for the duration). I managed to find a free parking spot about three blocks from where they were staying. This took the sting out of the hospital parking. I had dinner with them before returning home.

It has never been, and never will be easy work!
But the road that is built in hope
is more pleasant to the traveller
than the road built in despair,
even though they both lead to the same destination.

Marion Zimmer Bradley (1930–1999)

I had an early-evening appointment the next day, which meant that I would be able to park behind the hospital. I was at peace, feeling so much better about everything, even though my skin was blistered, peeling, and still quite red. The moistures and cortisone cream helped take the sting from the burns.

I was also quite tired with appointments all over the place.

I worked the following two days. I was getting stabbing pains more often now. I wore a scarf around my neck to protect the burns, which covered quite a large area. My throat was feeling swollen; food and drink sometimes goes up the back of my nose due to swallowing difficulty caused by the radiation. A large area of my body was being treated.

On 13 June, my appointment was late in the evening, so I was able to do housework and laundry before setting off. I parked behind the hospital. I was at peace and relaxed and getting to know a couple of other patients; having someone to converse with made it a bit more bearable,.

It was as though I was now coping very well, as I had remained bubbly and cheerful. I noticed that I may have been a bit too cheerful for some of the other patients and had to contain myself a little.

The next day, Tuesday, I had my sixteenth treatment and a doctor's appointment in the late afternoon. I had planned to do a quick trip to the supermarket, but with a flat battery, I had to wait for the call-out crew to change the battery. It was over an hour before they arrived, leaving it too late to go. I simply thanked God that I was at home when it happened.

I had a mid-morning appointment on 15th June; I took a relaxed drive to the free car park and then took the bus to the hospital. I noticed that one of the radiotherapists wore a compression garment on her arm; this meant that she had been through what I'm going through. I now knew that at least one person on the staff can relate to how the patients feel. She noticed that I was looking at the compression garment, I simply smiled at her.

I had plenty of friendly chatter with the other patients who liked my home made head wear. They examined my handy-work saying what a professional job I had done. Thank God, I was finally relaxed and at peace, thank God also for Thomas inspiring me as to how to relax, just by being as carefree as any child. Each day, I had more and more blisters, as the older ones burst and peeled new ones took their place. I picked up something to cook for dinner on my way home.

The following day was an early-afternoon appointment. I kept on the look-out for Thomas and his mother. Though I had not seen them, the white squares on the poster were being filled, one at a time. I asked the staff, and they told me how old he was. I told them how he had helped me emotionally.

On Friday, 17 June, I went shopping on my way to the hospital, as I had an early evening appointment. I hunted for a present to give Thomas. I wanted to get a dog, as I felt he must like dogs because of the poster. It couldn't be just any dog. I kept going back to a Scooby Doo dog with a walkie-talkie and decided that had to be it.

> *Acceptance of what has happened is the first step to overcoming the consequences of any misfortune.*
>
> *William James (1842–1910)*

I worked Saturday and Sunday wearing a scarf to protect my neck and to hide the burns. I wasn't too busy at work, making for a pleasant two days. I very happily got in and focused on what had to be done. Sadly, I was still not tolerating some foods. I was able to eat some things, but others still caused nausea.

I had an early-evening appointment for my twentieth treatment. After doing the laundry and some housework, I set off for the hospital.

My skin was constantly peeling and forming new blisters. My toenails caused a lot of pain, especially with my shoes on, and at night, I would catch the bedding. I cut off as much of the nail as possible and then used the Dr. Scholl file to gently grind the nail smooth. The stabbing pains due to the radiation continued, as did my sweaty back, which made me feel even colder, especially in the wintery breeze.

Keep heart …
to endure is greater than to dare;
to tire out hostile fortune;
to be daunted by no difficulty,
to keep heart when all have lost it –
who can say this is not greatness?

William Makepeace Thackeray (1811–1863)

Being Tuesday, I again had a doctor's appointment and treatment in the late afternoon. I drove and took the bus for the last part of the trip to the hospital. With having befriended several patients, I found plenty to talk about between doing crossword puzzles. I felt that I was being carried by angels; I felt very, very light.

I had to be up early the next day for an early appointment; I made my way through peak hour traffic to park and then took the bus the last part of the journey. I told the staff that I had a present for Thomas and wondered if our paths would cross again. They were curious as to why I was giving him a present. I told them that he was so brave and had given me inspiration as to how to cope. It was my way of thanking the little fellow.

Since I got home early, I was able to catch up on much needed rest.

The next day was an early evening appointment, giving me time to do some laundry. Chatting with the patients I had befriended there, made the wait for treatment more enjoyable. While conversing enables one to not dwell so much on the treatment.

I left the gift for Thomas with the staff, including my name and number on a card; after a few days, a phone call came. We arranged to meet at the hospital.

Meeting Mother and Boy

I had my twenty-fourth treatment on Friday; I had an hour with the physio before my lunchtime appointment. Before seeing the physio, I met Thomas and his mother. We talked for about half an hour. We had hugs and high-fives before he went to treatment and myself to physio. His mum gave me a big hug.

The next day, 25 June, was Maree's birthday. Now on annual leave, I went over for lunch although I was still eating poorly and having difficulty in swallowing.

The physio had told me to get some elastane vests to help move the lymphedema from my chest; I purchased a couple on the way home. I went to the markets on Sunday for fresh air and a visit to the staff at the spiritual shop (My Spirit) at old Petrie village. I picked up some information about a Reiki/SKHM workshop in October. The exact date and venue not yet confirmed.

Monday, 27 June, was my last radiation treatment. As I approached the desk to check in for the last time, I was singing, "Happy last day to me, happy last day to me."

I got up early to pick up Leigh, who would be staying the first week of the school holidays. We parked in the hospital car park.

She had cried the last time she stayed with me, so I asked the staff if they would show her around and explain what happens. They were fabulous with her.

Before we left, I gave the staff chocolates and thanked them for everything.

Out of every crisis comes the chance to be reborn, to conceive ourselves as individuals, to choose the kind of change that will help us to grow and to fulfil ourselves more completely.

Nena O'Neill (1923–2006)

Post-Treatment

On 28 June, Leigh and I played cards and a board game before we went to visit my surgeon for my sixth-month check-up. I wasn't thinking very clearly and wanted to head out the door before the appointment was over. I simply needed a break from being poked and prodded from all angles by all the different doctors. It would be great to be able to board a plane and just go on holiday. On the way home, we stopped at the play area of a park for an hour or so.

The next day, I woke with the vomits. The stabbing pains were coming and going as before, and I was sweating across my upper back. I slept poorly due to the pain and not being able to get a comfortable position.

I took Leigh to the movies, which was a fabulous distraction. We saw *Alice through the Looking Glass*.

Each day, the pain seemed more intense; it kept me awake. Late Friday evening, the nausea returned. The pain was more intense; I had rigors and a temperature of 37.8°C.

I could not get comfortable due to pain. My skin was blistered and broken, with some deep peeling and fluid build-up. I also had some difficulty in swallowing.

I was very tired when Alex came Saturday morning, bringing Xander with him. He pruned some trees; the grandchildren helped to remove some branches. After Alex mowed the lawn, they all returned home.

Early Monday morning, I rang the radiation clinic to inform them about the past few days. They told me to go to the nearest emergency department. I was kept in for the day while a series of tests were done. I was no longer able to use my left arm for blood tests due to the surgery/lymphedema, and the veins in my right arm had collapsed due to chemo; it proved a task getting samples of blood.

Apart from fluid build-up on the chest wall and arm, plus some swallowing issues, everything else had resolved, though I still had a cough that came and went. As I was leaving, the doctor told me to also check in with my GP, who prescribed analgesia.

In addition to being my birth month, July also marked the anniversaries of four very special people who died between the 7 and 20 (my birthday was the 12th); with the past several months taking a toll on me, I was quite emotional.

I was still weak and unable to do much; this seemed to be lasting ever so long. Getting tired easily seemed to last forever; it took its toll on me. Some days, I was just so sick and tired of everything that I broke down crying.

I started to process all that had happened, with time alone to reflect. It was all starting to hit home. The angels carried me the past eight-plus months—now I was free to feel, and it hurt much worse than before.

My emotions were all over the place, big time. I rang Ula, Leonie, Anne, Kate and Lynn and thanked them for their support. The past months had been relentless with appointments and treatments. The treatment seemed to drag at the time, going from one day to the next; now the time seemed to have flown. The angels really were carrying me.

I could still only tolerate a bland diet but found something at the noodle takeaway that I could tolerate occasionally.

On my way to Maree's, I followed a car speeding along with a trailer of gravel. The trailer hit a pothole, and gravel flew out, landing in the road and then hitting my car, leaving me with a badly chipped windscreen. More expense, the last thing I need, so took the car to the windscreen repairer. A windscreen had to be ordered in, to arrive the following day. The tyres needed replacing also, so I had both jobs done (an expense I could have done without) though I felt a lot safer with the jobs complete. These additional expenses impacted on my financial and mental stress during my recovery.

Mike and I ate out to celebrate the end of treatment.

Tuesday, my birthday, I went to the shopping mall, as I didn't want to sit around the house. I had lunch at the Vietnamese. There were flowers at the door when I got home, and more came over the next few days. It was starting to look like a florist; I loved it.

Visited Maree's mother-in-law Rita on Wednesday. The day before would have also been her mother's birthday; she had died four months earlier.

I drove to the free car park and then took a bus to the hospital for my afternoon physio appointment. Fluid still needed to be massaged from my upper arm and chest wall. I was unable to do my back due to old shoulder injuries. It is also very tiring, leaving me feeling annoyed and frustrated with myself. And although my cough was not too bad, it persisted.

The fluid gave me the feeling that something was wedged under my arm from the back. It felt tight around my arm, chest, and shoulder; I also had some cording of the muscles, causing more pain. I was simply exhausted.

I had morning tea with one of my work colleagues, Lynn (she had been through the surgery fourteen-plus years earlier). It was great to be able to express my feelings freely, knowing that she had an understanding.

The compassionate person understands that there is a time for talk and a time for silence.

Pablo Casals (1876–1973)

Dream 4 (Lesson 8)

I had a dream seeing myself with both breasts off. I knew that was what my surgeon wanted to do because of my family history, but I didn't feel up to it. She booked me in for a mammogram in November; this must have been on my mind when I fell asleep. I may have it done eventually, when I have recovered from all of the treatment. I'm still waiting on genetic testing as well. At the moment, though, I can't get my head around it. It is all too much to think about.

My emotions were still all over the place. I expect it was due to so much happening then into a void: wondering, always wondering, what now? I could do with a win on lotto so that I could retire; that would answer a lot of my prayers.

I was back to work on 23 and 24 July. I had kept up with some mandatory training on the e-learning website during breaks. My toes were painful with all the walking around on the wards, due to my toenails. On getting home, I did what I could to cut and grind my toenails so that they were not so painful with my shoes on.

I went to work on Tuesday, 26 July, with a big bag of chocolates. It was my first time without a hat—my hair was only one centimetre long—so it took a few minutes for the staff to recognise me. I gave the chocolates to Ashley to share around with all the staff and then went to see if I could organise a function, as I still felt the need to give back. After checking with the CEO, a function was organised for Tuesday, 2 August.

I worked 29, 30, and 31 July. Two patients commented on my hair. The first asked me if I was a "skin head." Being naïve to what that meant, I asked Anne. After hearing the explanation, I was puzzled as to why I was asked the question.

The other chap asked why I had my hair cut so short. I revealed my story, and then he proceeded to tell me of his experience with radiation for his prostate.

I caught up on more mandatory e-learning during breaks. My toenails were still giving me grief.

I went to work on 2 August for the function that I had organised for my colleagues. Catering/administration were very kind to charge wholesale prices. After lunch, I thanked everyone for their support and gave special thanks to others who had helped me in their free time. All well received.

Dream 5 (Lesson 9)

I had a dream where I was with a lot of dogs of all shapes, sizes, and colours. There were three very large light-coloured dogs and an extra-large black dog, all competing to be closest to me. I felt a little nervous, as they were leaning on me.

I feel this dream was telling me that management and staff appreciated what I did in return for what they did for me.

I went to Maree's on Wednesday. Xander wanted my attention a bit more than usual. Alex had been on several business trips lately, so I guess he thought he may get some extra attention from me.

I worked on 5 and 6 August, getting more of my e-learning done during breaks. The ward was quite busy, with a lot of running between the two wards; thankfully, my toenails were not as painful as before. We, more often than not had to run between the two wards.

I was up very early on Tuesday, 9 August, making my way through the peak hour traffic. I parked in the free car park and then took a bus to the hospital. It all had a very different feel with not having to have treatment; I sighed and relaxed. My radiation oncologist reviewed my progress and noticed that I still didn't have a compression garment/sleeve. All was going well, and I managed to get away early.

I had to have blood tests before my appointment with the medical oncologist. I had this done at work before my shift started. After three attempts, she had just one millilitre. I could feel the veins close off as she drew back on the plunger of the syringe. I told her that it was causing pain. She put the blood in paediatric tubes, and luckily, it was sufficient.

I also needed a bone density scan before the appointment. This was to measure the thickness of bone on a section of the hip and spine. This is a non-invasive procedure, taking no more than half an hour. I had lost a lot of my bone density.

A repeat of the pelvic ultrasound also had to be done to check for possible changes. All the pushing and shoving was quite painful. The cyst was no bigger than it was in December but three times the size that it was in June 2009. This would be removed after I recovered from all the treatment thus far.

I was still having difficulty swallowing. The cough persisted, as did my aching bones. The medical oncologist was late, having been delayed at a previous venue. We had a long talk. A lot of things had been troubling me. He explained everything ever so gently, telling me that my results were good. He commenced me on **oral** chemo and gave me a prescription. He said that it would no doubt make my bones ache even more, but he encouraged me to persevere.

He suggested that I consume plenty of dairy (which I was) plus take a supplement of vitamin K_2 + D_3 to aid the building of bone density. Supplements of omega-3 and turmeric are also good for joint pain. I queried the omega-3 but he reassured me saying that it was now time to use it.

The Pharmacist interviewed me for a lengthy period before making up my prescription as there is an extensive list of side effects which are quite severe. Should I get any of these severe side effects, I must inform the pharmacy and the doctor immediately.

Puss came into the bedroom. I had hoped for a sleep-in, but it wasn't to be. She called a few times to wake me. I looked down and to my dismay saw a dead bird. She looked at me, called out again, and left me with the dead bird. I thought to myself, That's fine for now, and went back to sleep.

I then had a dream. In the dream, Puss had come back with another gift. This time, she put it in my bed near my chest. I was horrified. When I took a look, it was a cute little kitten, calling to me. I woke with a fright, realising that it was just a dream. It was 5.30 in the morning. I fed her, then while she was eating, I disposed of the dead bird.

On reflection, I can see that she had put me in charge of her soul for keeping. I now feed her before I go to bed (which is usually late), hoping not to have a repeat.

My hair was slowly getting longer. I noticed that I had hair on my back; this was when I put heat packs on my back to help with back pain. It was like a waxing to remove them. I also noticed extra hair on my arms and cheeks (like sideburns). I hoped it wasn't permanent.

I did exercises prior to the lymph massage. All my lymph glands were massaged first to give them the stimulation required. Then gentle strokes across the upper chest followed the drainage system, then down the sides, going around my scar.

The fluid was massaged up my arm and then down my chest wall. While at rest, keeping your arm in an elevated position will also aid in fluid drainage.

Exercises as per the physiotherapist were gradually increased to regain strength and full range of movement. Always checking with my physio if any queries.

While the swallowing difficulty persisted, I found it much easier to have a soft to very soft diet. Often, I drank a lot of water for the food to go down. Leafy vegetables tend to get caught in the throat, even very small pieces. I usually took medication with yoghurt.

Life could not continue;
without throwing the past into the past,
liberating the present from its burden.

Paul Tillich (1886–1965)

After having been through such a harrowing experience, I was more than ready for an escape to someplace nice, where I could do as I please: a change in energy fields, with happy, healthy vibes.

With the effects of treatment expected to last a couple of years and emotions all over the place, some days I just crumbled. I felt it was more than I could cope with. I really needed a break away, far out of this area so that I could disconnect properly.

I was easily fatigued. I felt exasperated and often started to cry. I wanted to do things, but simply couldn't, as I ran out of "puff." Exercise is one of the treatments for cancer, which was why I was more than happy to do what I do. It's just that when I needed to rest, I needed to rest. Otherwise, I'd get filled with anxiety, and there is no place for anxiety in any cancer treatment. If I was at home, I just laid down and had a nap.

Still with the upcoming workshop on my mind I went and paid for it. The weekend workshop with SKHM Master Patrick Zeigler would help me relax and be at peace, to reinvigorate my very being. I contacted Chris, Kim and Pam who I had not seen so much in past year. I put a mat and cushion aside for this workshop. I also purchased extra fruit and bottled water for the event. I was very excited and so looking forward to the experience of the weekend.

My stomach had been bloated; some days, more than others. I got quite "windy" with it: both ends, making all sorts of noises. Mike referred to me as a "one-man musical band." It was an embarrassment to go anywhere.

Puss had settled in so well that it seemed she had always been here. We seem to know the expectations of each other.

Andrew had driven the fifteen hundred-plus kilometres from far north Queensland, staying with me a few days before heading to their Nancy's for Grace's christening. An old friend of mine in Western Australia died that same weekend. This saddened me greatly as the effects of chemo had put him into organ failure.

I was now able to wear the car seat belt the correct way. I went to my GP for a review because of my bloating; it can have many causes, some more sinister than others. I needed to put my mind at ease. My pelvic ultrasound was unchanged since December. I also wanted to know my blood results, the actual results, and so I went over them with my GP.

The cancer marker was negative: big sigh of relief (but I still required the maintenance chemo tablets – possibly for five years). My liver functions were a bit out; this explained the yellow tinge of my skin, plus the wind and bloating. It would take several more months before the IV chemo was filtered through the liver. Liver functions have to be normal before any further surgery can be done; we aimed for the end of the year.

My emotions started to subside immediately, though I did want that cyst gone already. On booking an appointment for November's mammogram, I was very surprised to learn that there was no free screening for anyone who has had a diagnosis and treatment of breast cancer; that was now a thing of the past.

I finally got a compression sleeve on 20 September; hallelujah!

Now I would be able to get out of Brisbane for a break, to get away from this madness. Oh, to be free, if only temporarily; I only got as far as Dan and family overnight (I needed to gradually build up how far I could drive).

I had changed to a physio closer to home so that I wouldn't be travelling long distances all the time.

To wear a compression sleeve, you remove your rings, pull it over your wrist, and then put a rubber kitchen glove on other hand (as it has grips); next, using the glove, you ease the compression sleeve into place (the glove protects the garment from fingernails so as to not destroy the elastin). With just one garment and it costing so much, it needed good care.

The more active I am, the more lymphedema is an issue; the physio suggested I wear the compression sleeve and a compression vest while driving, travelling, and working.

Maintaining good drainage is also aided by regular massaging and elevation. Compression garments to remain in situ for two hours after getting back into my normal, regular routine. I still get fluid build-up, regardless.

I may still have the aches and pains and cough when I went somewhere, but I could actually go now. It felt like a weight was off my shoulders. I could have gone to my friend's funeral in W.A. had I had the sleeve.

I was still eating poorly, unable to tolerate some foods, and unable to swallow others. I had trouble swallowing and needed a lot of fluid to wash food down.

With emotions and doubts settled, I was relaxed into healing. I looked forward to new blood vessels and lymph vessels forming (especially the lymph vessels, as then I wouldn't have to massage them as often).

Recovering from all the invasive treatment: that was where I was, with never-ending future appointments.

Phone calls and letters from those unable to be near proved to be of great support. The book that Ula gave me plus all my own spiritual books managed to pull me through, with a bit of a struggle. I don't know how others have managed without the support of family or friends or a spiritual way of life; it has been my saving grace. I have several thousand-piece jigsaw puzzles which keep my mind busy also; the few I have are quite a challenge.

I would definitely never wish anything like this on anyone at all. There has to be a less barbaric treatment—surely.

I will forever be grateful for the deep meaningful words that I found to be so healing. I had been finding it difficult to go past the place where I had treatment; as time goes on, this lessens. Working in a hospital and then having treatment at a hospital, I feel, added to my need to get away. I felt no solace.

One of my earlier patients and his partner came into work, bringing me a huge bouquet of flowers, a gift, and beautiful card, which had me laughing on and off for hours due to the words written in the card. It was so very touching and brought a tear to my eyes.

He had said that I got him out of a dark place; his personally thanking me in this way, got me in a better frame of mind.

Memories take you back, but dreams take you forward.

H.G. Wells (short version)

My personal struggles continued in the following months. The excess hair was now gone; thank God for that. The hair on my head was much thicker, like it was when I was younger. The colour and texture remained the same though.

My diet improved; I ate a little more but was still unable to eat some things or to swallow other things; therefore, I was still taking supplements.

I had an appointment with my surgeon on 10 November 2016; with all going well and looking good, I was given a referral to another surgeon to do the next procedure.

I had an appointment with the surgeon 21 November; with all in order, a date was made for surgery. I wanted it done before Christmas so that 2017 would be completely free of treatment. Our ward was busy until Christmas for the seasonal closure; 22 December was the date scheduled for surgery: laparoscopic surgery for both ovaries and fallopian tubes to be removed (my appendix was also to be removed).

I received the VIP treatment from the admissions desk, through the theatre, to recovery, and to the ward.

Christmas came and went, followed by a heat wave for the New Year. I relied on Mike to take me places until I was permitted to drive (I could drive eleven days after surgery).

The surgeon called on 4 January with all tests clear; all specimens were free of cancer cells. The left ovary and tube had endometriosis, the right ovary and tube had fibroma, the appendix was clear, and the abdominal washings were clear.

It was a New Year and a new beginning.

I hoped to slow down a little by being on a less busy ward. I would lead the way by asking, though I may be scared to do so.(yet another unknown) I was happy to accept the fact that I was not as agile as I once was. I was happy to move to the next phase of my life, daunting as it may feel.

Reflections

I know now that I had been frozen with fear during the treatment. Fear can help you survive potentially dangerous situations. Sometimes, fear can prevent you from facing challenges, from meeting new people, and from broadening your horizons. My fear simply had me in a state of paralysis.

We add to our fear by trying to appear strong and then worrying that how we really feel will be found out; otherwise, we could simply give up and retreat into our own world.

Fear may intensify into panic or terror when we intellectualise it or disassociate. I'm not sure how bad I got; other people were showing concern, though.

I showed myself, warts and all. At times, I felt safe to do so, but not always, as it happened at inopportune times.

My father often told me that I was afraid of my own shadow; I can say that I am now more comfortable with it. I have been forced to make the dark and uncomfortable bits my friends, my allies. A renewed closeness to Mike has come from this darkness. Better understanding with friends and family has been my reward.

Once I may have trusted in another to treat me in the correct manner; now, I trust in my own love and respect for myself, which determines how I let others treat me.

As the saying goes, no pain, no gain. It is also said that to ride a bicycle, one has to keep moving, or else fall off. Well, I kept moving through the pain, and yes, I did gain in so many ways.

With moving comes growth. Growth spiritually, mentally, and physically, thus becoming a better person through the little steps and the big ones, also. I feel I am not yet done; I feel a new destination on the horizon. This time, I won't be getting a push.

Life responds to movement, though few people move until they are in pain from being too rigid. They become stuck in their conditioning, their comfort zones.

Over the years, I have heard it said that I had changed. Initially, it went unnoticed; I just saw myself as learning and expanding. Now that I look back, I acknowledge what was said as I, too, now see and feel it. I have simply stopped living life from their perspective.

Personally, I do not base my self-worth on what others think (though it was important once). When I once lived with someone (long ago in another life-time) I had felt so alone, as it was then fashionable to worry about what others may think. That may sound judgemental; it is human to err, after all.

Healthy anger is essential to happiness, something which I have had to express. Anger is only unhealthy when a low self-worth is in question; yes, I was angry about my situation at times, due mostly to frustration of not being able to be as I had been when I was healthy.

Finding the quiet within had been an issue, our inner being our outer foundation. The peace being the master of the restlessness; we can travel all day yet go no place at all when going within. For myself, though, I really needed a change of energy—what some call vibes—and to simply remove myself from that field. It was the only way I knew how to nurture myself.

I have shown who I am outwardly and what I felt inwardly, warts and all, as embarrassing as that may be.

Now, my heart content, I feel the joy and freedom to express an entire range of emotions without separation of good and bad and being free to release my emotions.

All emotions are intrinsically pleasurable. When you resist feeling what is, you experience pain. This pain is the blocked energy. Energy wants to be in motion; just as the river wants to flow. Blocked energy is the source of depression and disease (dis-ease, not being at ease).

We don't have to change who or what we are; we simply have to be aware of all our projections, whether it be greed or anger allowing delusion to evaporate.

I am so glad that I am able to connect and stay with inner peace again. It was as though a part of me was missing. It actually had me feeling lonely—something I hadn't felt in a long while. Today, I feel alive and light-hearted; thank God. I accept that during the past year, I have not really liked myself or what I was having to deal with. I also accept that I have not been proud of what I said or did. I accept it all because it made me who I am now. Some may think of life as a massive stack of problems, but surely, these problems are but mystery upon mystery, waiting to be solved. After all, we are spiritual beings, having human experiences. This is why it is enjoyable seeking new friends and discovering the newness life has to offer.

Even the Dalai Lama says that fear is necessary. Positivity does not mean passive acceptance. Wisdom notes all aspects of reality, but with strong fearful or disturbing emotions, we cannot see this.

Hardship can, and often does, lead to stress and depression. We need to be able to muster up and cultivate calm, adaptability, and insight to find a loving kindness, regardless of what else may be happening.

A specific state of mind is required; it is trying to recognise a change in thought before it escalates. Tai chi breathing helps to calm the thought process before panic sets in. Notice how your thoughts can make you think, feel, act, and interact. Recognising what these habits do, allows you to begin to reduce their hold on you. It takes brain energy to do this initially: putting focus on your thought process. You then follow into and through this illusion, as it no longer has a hold on you. This makes you in charge of your thoughts as you progress in the shift from the negative thought process.

In theory, the brain rewires bit by bit; each time, you intentionally make a shift. The more you do this, the stronger it becomes, making it easier each time.

You may have repeated less desirable thoughts thousands of times, but re-education of the thought process (if you are consistent) will bring a positive outcome.

Staying mindful of yourself allows you to become more immune to the pull of negative thoughts.

The main theme is to remain aware of all things; focus on breathing.

Early in my treatment, I chose to walk the avoidance path. Avoidance distances you from strong emotions, fearing of being overwhelmed. Eventually, you are able to confront your fears and be open to your emotions.

A gardener may dedicate all the best conditions for a garden; it will then flourish. We simply do the same for ourselves.

You can't force yourself to be calm, but you can be open to being calm; this is the beginning. If you repeat it enough, it will become a habit. To break a habit, stay aware of the possibilities and whatever comes and goes in your mind; neither focus on it nor suppress it. Just observe it.

The problem begins with unconscious cause-and-effect sequences: conditioned suffering. Since we learnt these habits, they can be unlearnt.

Each annoying thought that runs through your mind can get you hooked, or you can let it go and take charge.

First, practice letting go of the small things, making it much easier to let go of the bigger things.

Awareness can help you to nip it in the bud before it escalates. Emotions can seem permanent or frozen in time; just as ice melts, you too can allow yourself to let go of unhealthy thoughts.

Being mindful clears your perception and opens the way to change, whether it has to do with fear, binging, or other learned habits or negative thought forms.

It is learning to be respectful of yourself amid whatever else may be going on.

Looking back on my treatment from a mindful perspective, I would say that I truly felt like prey while the predators—the staff simply doing their job—did the treatment. This will make me even more mindful in my work.

If you are unaware of a particular thought or mood or mode, even though you may have resolved the issue at hand, you continue on the same path, resolving issues until you reach that moment when you recognise it for what it is.

Buddha had said: To know the path, one must become the path. This had me bewildered when I initially read it, though I now understand the meaning. The experience of such a long illness/treatment has lead me to realize that to understand something, one must experience it themselves. (standing in the shoes of the other person)

I finally took myself to a place where the energy feels as though it fits like the glove out in nature. I travelled through the mountains and national parks, absorbing al the energy from the trees, mountains, rocks, rivers, creeks, and all the creatures from birds and butterflies to lizards, fish, and tortoises. All this can be found in nature, far away from suburbia and the hustle and bustle, the madness of it all. What peace, what joy. I was elated; my spirit soared, and my heart sang. I was free.

I found myself a pair of gardening boots while on my travels. There is a pattern on them: little sheep all over the boots with the words "sheep happens" between the sheep.

Yes: Sheep does happen!

"This too shall pass …"
I was taught these words by my grandmother
(as a phrase that is to be used at all times in your life.)

When things are spectacularly dreadful;
when things are absolutely appalling;
when everything is superb and wonderful and marvellous and happy …

Say these words to yourself.

They will give you a sense of perspective and help you also to make sense of what is good and to be stoical about what is bad.

Claire Rayner (1931–)

Afterward

On 12 April 2017 I have an appointment with the geneticist. This will be helpful information for the extended family. My cousin Jane was tested after her mastectomy; she does not have the mutation. In my heart of hearts, I know that I also, do not have the mutation in my genes.

Oral chemo has increased the pain in my body, it aches to the point where I lay awake for hours. As the weeks and months went by there were many times that I felt to stop treatment. My bones were grating and felt to be falling to pieces. My joints were popping in and out of joint 'willy-nilly'; my nervous system felt to be burning – on fire. I was having spasms and cramps; my memory came to the stage that caused me concern; I felt to be choking and unable to swallow. I was spilling things, dropping things. I felt that I was wrapped in hot coals filled with needles. When I walked, I felt that I was walking on hot nails. The pain shot down my spine through to my feet. All these symptoms of pain caused severe headaches leaving me constantly weak and tired.

I still have a mortgage. I don't wish to die this way.

I stopped my treatment on 14 Feb. 2017. This was my own personal, conscious decision; which I feel is right for me.

It took almost four weeks before having a clear mind – I must admit that I started to have my doubts as the pain persisted. I passed gallons of urine in that time, my joints started to settle. As my mind became clear, the aches and pains etc. began to ease also. I was now able to eat much better, swallow without choking as often. This is when I came across a study from 2012 in U.S.A. Instantly, I knew I was doing the right thing. Synthetic THC (cannabis compound) destroyed incurable cancer. Not all patients are informed that chemo tends to cause other cancers and heart conditions, nor are they told that radiation can also lead to other cancers. The poor diet consumed during treatment can also lead to other health issues – we are all informed that bad eating habits lead to cancer and health issues. A cycle that I am gradually able to remove myself from. I have started eating raw fruit/veg. when I am able. Some foods still cause nausea and vomiting since having chemo.

I pray that it doesn't remain with me as it has with Aunt Elsie.

In my reflections, I noted that current treatment is barbaric. Seeing the U.S.A. study where a patient was given synthetic THC for a brain tumour has given me hope for future sufferers. This treatment was recently legalised. It is not too far from being reality in Australia also having been legal since 1 March 2017 though we need the actual treatment at hand for the doctors to prescribe it.

In the study of history, we see all the barbaric things done. This is how I relate to chemo and radiation, especially that doctors manage to convince people to swallow poison – chemo.

Those 'at high risk' are encouraged to have mammograms six monthly and MRI yearly – all radiation. The contrast for MRI can lead to brain cancer.

"How Could Anyone Ever Tell You" – song by Julie Felix reminds us that, regardless of what we have endured, we are beautiful/loveable.

About the Author

Heather Macdonald was born in 1952 in Tully, a small country town in North Queensland, Australia. Both of her parents instilled in her a sense of spirituality, and at a young age she was interested in alternative styles of healing. Heather is a single mother and works as a registered nurse, and she also practices spiritualism as a Reiki master and Seichim master.

Printed in the United States
By Bookmasters